# Life's Mixed Poetry

# Books by the Anonymous Author and Artist

*Life's Novellas: Fate Waits Upon No One*

The good and the bad are juxtaposed, chronologically, fictionally, and theatrically.

*Their Poetic Minds*

Poems are juxtaposed, religiously, femininely, and dichotomously.

*Poems of Life*

Poems are mixed schematically, stylistically, and randomly.

*Life's Heart Break: A Novella*

In the end, will Zenald discover one of life's biggest heart-aches: heart-break?

*Duty & Destruction I*

A real female experiences life in and out of the U.S. military.

*Life's Poetic Dichotomies*

Some of life's biggest dichotomies are juxtaposed poetically.

*Her Poetic Rise*

It is for the religiously poetic that blends religion and feminism.

*Life's Short Stories*

Fictional characters vie to live their own lives.

# Art Book

*The Diamond & Heart Art Collections*

Pictures are exhibited, categorically, by coloring schemes and coloring mediums; all of which, have been affected with special effects.

Schemes: pastel shades; earth tones; primary colors; gray, black and white; black and white.

Mediums: colored pencils; water coloring; pastel coloring; acrylic coloring; oil coloring.

# Life's Mixed Poetry

Anonymous

Century Conquests

# *Life's Mixed Poetry*

Copyright © 2011 by Anonymous

All rights reserved. Printed in the United States of America. No part of this book may be used or reproduced in any way, at all, without written permission from the publisher, except, in the case of brief quotations embodied in critical articles or reviews.

www.centuryconquests.com
info@centuryconquests.com

ISBN: 978-0-9850698-4-1

Cover graphic designed by: Century Conquests © 2011

Century Conquests ® 2012

# Life's Mixed Poetry

Anonymous

# Acknowledgements

For the small voice deep inside me that wants me, all over again, to carry on poetically.

I thank everyone that has helped with the publication of this book.

I even thank every single reader of my book for indulging my mixed brand of poetry and all that it entails.

It is a bad plan that admits of no modification.

—*Publilius Syrus*
(42 B.C.)

# Part 1

# Changes

                    Changes….

Changes...?                                                  Changes!

                    Changes….

Changes!                                                  Changes…?

                  Changes are coming….

Changes…?

                    Changes….

                                                Changes…!

Yes, changes are coming—without change every thing stays the same.

                    But nothing stays the same;

              Since every single thing almost always changes.

Oh yes! Changes and changes and ev'n more changes….

## Oneness

I almost always seek to have a measure of it—Peace;
Yet, it's what almost certainly keeps peace at bay—workaholic beast.

## Picture of the Lady

The lady is standing in the center of the overly open and greenish-gold-colored field.
Fruit trees are plentiful as are the vegetable plants that are sprouting from its rich soil.
    The lady's petite but lean yet firm body suggests her toil on the farm-land.
        Her face is somewhat visible under a wide sun hat.
Under it, her long and strawberry-colored hair is blowing in the freshly countrified air.
She's conscious of the big fire-ball that is just hanging in the cobalt-blue-colored sky.
    Still, under that widely big hat—it, I see some of her beautiful face:
        Its delicate features; creamy complexion; healthy glow….
Her great big smile is even suggesting how very happy she is with her rustic life and all.
    Doesn't her hackneyed and dull denim, out-fit—or, cover-alls,
        Even suggest a pretty plain picture of this lovely lady's life?

## "Today, I start to change my life," speaks the poetic character.

Character: Today, I start to change my life.
Me: Why today of all days…?

Character: Well, today's as good as any other day.
Me: How right you are.

Me: Really, why've you chosen today, especially, to change your life?
Character: Actually, I've needed to make some serious changes in my life for a very long time.

Me: Oh?
Character: Yeah, for I'm done being a real—no-good-for-nothing—do-nothing…!

Me: How'll you change?
Character: Haw, I've since gotten some religion.

Me: What type of religion?
Character: Buddhism, of course.

Me: Why Buddhism?
Character: Because, I like what it represents, and, roundly.

Me: What does it represent?
Character: It's simple. Any suffering that I may've is because of my own desire. And, the only sure way to end it is through personal enlightenment.

Me: Uh-huh. Do you've a supportive system…?
Character: A what? Naw—I don't need one because I've my *own* damn power…!

Me: So, you're going it alone?
Character: That I am.

Me: Please, tell me, what's the "new you" looking to get in return for this so-called change…?
Character: Well, I'd like to see all of my deliciously good dreams come true and then stay true!

# Nature's Night

Thunder roaring
        Stars glimmering
                Fluffy clouds flying
                      One quarter of a moon standing guard
                              In a blackish-gray sky
                                      All a part of nature's night.
Lightning crackling
        Stars glowing
                Clouds vanishing
                      One-half of a moon standing guard
                              In a grayish-black sky
                                      All a part of nature's night.
Raindrops falling
        Stars shining
                Cotton-candy clouds floating
                      Three quarters of a moon standing guard
                              In a blackish-blue sky
                                      All a part of nature's night.
Ice crystals dropping
        Stars beaming
                Clouds passing
                      Full mid-night moon standing guard
                              In a bluish-black sky
                                      All a part of nature's night.

## A Heated Mess

Never mind—that, that wildly workaholic beast causes me such Pother;
I'm still inclin'd to follow it although the beast's path just gets much hotter and harder!

# The Master Seller
(A Found Poem)

Palm Beach Townhomes

    The Palm Beach Townhome Specialist

        Samora Satiny: Licensed Real Estate Broker/Agent

            3000 Royal Palm Way, Suite # 0003

                Palm Beach, Florida  33401

                    561.765.4321

                        www.SamoraSatiny.com

                            Samora@Hotmail.com

# The Un-Covering of a Soul

In the beginning…,

You caress'd my hand, circularly, and lovingly, and even supportingly.

A gesture of realness…?

…An imbroglio—or delusion and confusion:

Forms of some pretty perplexed punishment—or,

Un-speak-able and grief-stricken pain…!

A living incubus—harmful emotions—thoughts out of control;

Or, openly over-bearing feelings—or, even, malice and misery….

But, my days and nights are once again renascent;

Time—an awfully wonderful healer….

Intimate feelings that weren't factitious but really real.

Such extraordinary emotions—

An enormous burden having been lift'd: or, the un-covering of a soul.

…Deliciously or deliriously if not erotically happy.

Because, our colorfully circular love—so clear, yet colorful, and complete;

Still, we're almost, always, faithful, toward bringing each other much joy and pain.

## Life of Luxury

The ambitious female almost always earns her Success.

Neither should it be some great big marvel.

That she consciously, courageously, and certainly conquers life with much zest.

Don't be in-correct, either, by ev'r challenging her bravado.

Nev'r mind, too, that such female likes wearing a western-styled vest;

Because nothing could or would ev'r mess up her success—lest,

She stops wanting to be the very best: or, pass all of life's most difficult tests.

# Vital Spirit

Truly, whose is it, Life?

And, why doesn't his life have any strife?

Is it because of her: the man's wife?

It's also true that the two almost nev'r fight;

That's right, for the twosome almost always avoid some jagged knife.

They do so, too, ev'n, in the darkest of night.

Since, the brightly light-color'd couple aren't about any slight.

They're just too damn full of peace-making might!

That's right; the two wouldn't dream, financially, ev'r, of flavoring such a bite;

For they almost certainly can't afford such cost.

That is, neither he nor she wants to be the boss and suffer a great big loss!

# Part 2

# Dreams

Dreams, dreams…? Yes!

Dreams aren't only for those who sleep but ev'n for those who weep.

Dreams, dreams…? Yes, dreams!

The un-conscious mind awakes when the body falls asleep.

Drifting, drifting, and drifting right—along, into the utter un-known:

A place where the ordinary mind fails, fantastically, to register the deep and ev'n very deep wants, needs, and fears….

Dreams and bad dreams and ev'n nightmares speak for the un-conscious—or,

The sub-conscious mind….

Dreams…? Dreams! Yes, dreams.

Deep and ev'n very deep or deep and dark or ev'n very dark dreams….

Dreams—oh yes—dreams…!

## Physical Condition

Nothing is as important as her contractible Health—
Except, maybe, for her impendent death;
This is why she ought to distribute her darkly hard-won wealth.

# My Passionate Love

My Passionate Love, oh yes! My Passionate Love….
Only in my most desperate dream that I've envision'd, ev'r,
A love that's so divine; that, I'm bless'd beautifully to have found.
Before you came into my life, there was emptiness and loneliness:
Unfavorable feelings that often made me felt dead inside—or, so listless and lifeless;
Which has caus'd so much sadness and madness.
When, you *now* shower me with lasting lust, loyalty, and your passionate love;
Only, then, do my most treasur'd dream come true again and again.
A reality that you, or my Passionate Love have brought color, mirth, and so much joy to;
As you, or, my Passionate Love have erased the darkness; that's shroud'd,
Oh, such super shimmery sweetness—once dormant in my life.
Yes, indeed, I'm happy, and, haphazardly, that you—or, my Sweet Sugar are the one;
Who's since seiz'd and mend'd my broken heart.
Then, on that delightful day—or, your marriage proposal—and,
After much rapturous romance, I thank you—yes I do…!
For my world has turn'd around, since:
My life now seems as though it's a roundly romantic fairytale:
My being whirl'd round about in a circle of sunshine; the loveliest of spring flowers;
The sensuous scene of candle-light; a moony ocean; a prized incense; and,
The endless joy of knowing that we'd become parents.
A beautiful baby boy is now ours and has since shown us a sight of utterly un-told
Happiness!
When, I look lovingly at our precious child's eyes—my Passionate Love—oh yes!
My very Passionate Love, for I'm just bless'd most beautifully, all over again!

## Body Blow

The omniscient, omnipotent, arrogant, and condescending, and ev'n money-hungry male absolutely abhors any sort of failures.

Yet, his precariously puffy pride almost always causes him to make some errors.

        Still, he almost nev'r likes to Fail;

        If so, you'll almost certainly hear the male yell!

        Such makes it nearly impossible for him to ev'r find any kind of real mate;

        If so, she or he had better nev'r make any type of damned mistake!

# The Move
(Rush & Relax—Enjambment)

Come right to a stop and silence the engine;
      Get right out the car and right through the gate.

Get the key and open the door;
         Enter the house and throw right down your things.

Sit right on the sofa and kick right off your shoes;
           Settle right back and just relax a bit…!

## Bad Health

EEEK! The dark, dirty, and dangerous parasite likes visiting it upon her, Sickness.

That's right, and the male almost always visits the female at night.

Since darkness almost certainly conceals his wickedness.

# It's Just Another Year

Another year has come and gone:
A year that's given so much; yet, it's taken back ev'n more....
A year that's held such peace, health, love, and happiness, and even success.
Has it been only a fantastic, if not a fabulous figment of my imagination...?
Peace. Peace! Peace? Is it for sleepers that sleep peacefully—or, eternally?
Aren't peaceful promises made to be broken, prettily?
Superficial health—cheap, fleeting, and it oftentimes has the capacity to leave one weak.
But, true health is found only beneath the exterior;
It's the essence of the spirit that moves lives.
Then, why would those same lives disregard the way in which they've been thus moved?
Love is rather revocable;
It's impossible, possibly, to savor such state of condition, ev'r, when every time
one finds love—it turns right to heart-break.
Happiness is supposed to be, oh, so beautiful! Yet, when I stare at it, I see an utter
ugliness that won't disappear: That it's one-sided, stingy, and seemingly bad—yes, evil!
Perhaps, it's been only a damnably deceptive, or an utterly un-happy love; that, I've
been given unhappily or sweetly from the super sourness of destiny's heart....
A good year has visited, howev'r, not nearly enough:
Here, one year and long gone by the next year—why?
I ask again, why ... after all that's been paid, most prettily, in the price of pain and
suffering—or misery: persecution.
Another year has since come and gone.
It's been a year that's given so much; still, it's taken back ev'n more...;
A year that's promised and delivered:
Such peace and pother; health and sickness; love and heartache; happiness and sadness;
Success and failure; and, oh yes, so much joy and sorrow;
All of which, more than likely, will be right around tomorrow.

## Put Away

To the weak and foolish ways of man-kind, she'll almost nev'r submit.
>HOORAY!

To the strong and smart ways of woman-kind, she'll almost always Commit.
>It's how the woman prefers, exactly, to be portray'd.

To all those who dare question the woman's circular courage of convictions,
>Know this is something that she'll not, at all, permit.

To like her or dis-like her, it's quite simply your choice;

Remember, though, that the woman has a super strong voice that'll almost certainly be hoist from a most reliable source.

## Some Surrealism

My lover whose love is from an utterly un-lovely school;
Whose sight is like an old, cock-eyed, and un-insightful fool;
Whose hearing is like a black, deaf, and un-sharp bat;
Whose smell is like a dark, nasty, and smelly musk-rat;
Whose feel is like a cold, hard, and square cube of ice;
Whose taste is like burnt, dried-out, and dead mice.

## Mis-Obligation

The darkly monstrous-looking mis-fit and malingerer of a male is almost always moody.

And, why's that?

Well, maybe, it's because of his down-right Dereliction of Duty;

Instead of standing the military watch, he, almost, certainly, chooses, to linger, so aimlessly, like some wet, fat, and lazy rat.

That's correct, for the monstrously dark-looking malingerer and mis-fit of a male is an absolutely aim-less derelict, so truly.

This is why Uncle Sam aims, too, to degrade, and discard, and even disinherit the male of a malingerer, right away.

That's correct, as there's always a damn high price to pay. Quite simply, there'll be no more damn'd decay or rot on the watch neither today nor tomorrow or any other day. HURRAY!

.

# Part 3

# Talk to Me
(A Poem of Dialogue)

"You're feeble. So, how can I love you?"

"I know that I'm sometimes weak."

"You're feeble and foolish and I can't love you."

"I know that I'm sometimes un-wise but…."

"You're self-serving. So, tell me, how can I love you?"

"I know that I'm sometimes self-seeking and…."

"You're neglectful of yourself—and, me. I can't love you."

"I know that I'm sometimes un-comb'd—or, lackin'…."

"You're list-less—and, worth-less. So, please, just, tell me how can I love you?"

"I know that I'm sometimes use-less—but—"

"You're utterly un-lovable and I can't—or, won't ev'r love you!"

"I know that you can't—or won't ev'r love me, circularly, or roundly."

# The Surprise

Sky blue-black; streets empty;
    Crickets asleep; neighborhood quiet;
        The house looks inviting.

Step slowly; knock lightly;
    Listen carefully; wait impatiently;
        Somebody just has to answer the door.

Look surprisingly; ask politely;
    Listen intently; back up, slowly;
        Since that, somebody appears to my surprise.

Turn away; I'm embarrassed to say—
    That someone isn't supposed to be there—or, here;
        Yet, that somebody—oh well—hell!

I just can't believe it—and, I still don't believe it;
    I've to disappear into the black-blue night.
        However, quietly, for I'm surprised….

## Turtledove

When one finds it, how long does it last—Love?
> This is to say—or ask: Won't it eventually fly away like an adventurously
>> Adulterous dove?

Until I know such answer, for sure, I'll just sit and wait in my lovely, bubbly, and cuddly
> Tub....

It's where I often find a measure of love as oppos'd to a masculinely parasitic club.

# The Port

I'm just sitting here under the warmly Floridian sun and cloudily blue-gray sky.
    The wind's balmy breeze is blowing hard off the rough and deep Atlantic Sea.
    Tall and somewhat leafless trees are just rocking to and fro.
They're adding even more wind to an already windy and warm morning.
The traffic's now so very busy: cars coming and going or moving all about; buses just keep rolling in and out; picking up and dropping off plenty passengers; a police cruiser is policing the area, even: giving tickets quickly to all those failing to obey the port's
        Strict rules....
Not, exactly, out of the gray-blue, I hear her.
    It's the super shrill sound of some majestic ship sounding her loud horn.
    The ship is about to set sail for parts utterly un-known.
        And, some time after…, she's taken to the greenish-blue sea.
          I can see, clearly, her cruising rather gracefully.
Her color and size and even style and all now rule the bluish-green sea—so undoubtedly.

## Iron-Heartedness

Pretty please—just, call me Dave!
    Though, I must confess that such isn't my real name.
        Just the same, that the name or Dave could nev'r be in vain;
      It's because I'm almost always Brave!
        That I almost nev'r cave!
It's because I can't—or, won't allow my really good name, ev'r, to be maim'd!
      Since, I'll forev'r remain a part of life's damn'd dog-eat-snake—game!
      To be boldly brave, it's also almost certainly how I've to behave!

.

# The Place

It's a classy yet boisterous and sultry space of a place.

The exclusive community is ensconced amid a lush landscape and high brick walls.

The breezy wind is blowing—and, dead leaves are falling from tall trees.

The lighting is giving the scene a somewhat subdued look if not feel.

The bright buildings and stylish surroundings are all showing some class.

The community's residents appear or seem to be well-to-do.

The well-off people are even lounging around the big, empty, and cerulean-colored pool.

Most are just sitting about drinking, smoking, talking, and smooching, and even butt-watching.

Some are indulging the hot and bubbly Jacuzzi.

Others are absorbing both the steamy sauna's and the dry sauna's stifling humidity.

As if on cue, a handsomely tan-colored man dives right into the cerulean-colored pool.

He starts swimming some lengthy laps.

His muscular arms are ripping right through the wavy water with such flair, or finesse.

His hardened legs are even rising and falling rhythmically.

Now, the sound of music, foot-steps, and all, are reminding me that it's time for the night-life to begin, essentially, and most un-classily. HOOPLA!

# Some Dark Stranger

We met and then we talked then we became so-called friends;

    But, still, I don't know you.

We worked together and then we played together and even made some plans together;

    But, still, I don't know you.

We ate dinner together and then we went to a movie-theater together;

    But, still, I don't know you.

We didn't say good-bye and then we lost contact and even went our separate ways.

      And, to this day, I can say—only, that you're some nakedly dark stranger;

        Who, apparently, wanted only to have fun—together.

## Weighed Down

The man's dream has been to nev'r experience any true Heartache.
    Yet, life's full of necessary surprises, or rather, necessary disappointments;
Like a legitimately lovable, loyal, and love-sick lady who's been, of course, on the take.
So, the only thing that the woman and the man both should do is just accept their fates.
    Since, it's been more than just lent.

## Faint Heart

    The female could nev'r be some sourly power-less Coward.
Un-like some male or scaredy-cat that wants, instead, to hold her back or take her down.
    That is, nothing could—or, would ev'r make her glow'r and then cow'r.
    Because, she has such purplish-pink-color'd power:
It's the sort of tall, tone, and tangibly tight might—that, almost, always, keeps the righteously round female's power strongly bound.
    That's so right! She'll almost nev'r be held back or taken down;
      For the female's no weak or foolish clown—POUND!
She's once again wound—or, so duty-bound; right, to some powerful principles of life, and methodologies by which it ought to be liv'd: her damn life.
Nor is there any time to frown or be down, ev'r; since, the female intends to conquer the nakedly, if not the dangerously dark town. HORRAY!

## Eternal Rest

What's life's greatest test?
Is it where one ends up after Death?
No doubt, that such question ought not to be a subject for some idle chatter.
Why not? It's because death—it, almost, always, matters.
That is, whether one ends up in heaven or hell or ev'n some where in between is of great Consequence.
Since such will almost certainly exemplify one's life's significance.
Or better, would one much rather live one's life not according to some much higher principles of life and methodologies by which it ought to be lived; but, instead, according to one's own self-imposed, self-styled, and self-serving terms?
If so, pretty please, just, bear in mind—that, one alone will account for such:
One's own damned dark germs.

# Part 4

# My Un-Ending Enemy

I see you today just as I've almost always seen you:

    You're great in your own way but weak and wistful.

I see you today just as I've almost always seen you:

    You're attractive in your own way but sour and stationary.

I see you today just as I've almost always seen you:

    You're at ease in your own way but cold and connivent.

I see you today just as I've almost always seen you:

    You're quite simply my ev'r-lasting enemy…!

# Happy-Go-Lucky

The male comedian experiences such Happiness.

That is, never mind his lack of a fabulously factual life.

It's just that his colorful craft allows for much nakedness.

That's right, as he and his wife both likes to deal with circularly comical strife.

Because of such nakedness, the clownish comic manages to exhibit lots of wackiness.

# The Here and Now
(A Sense Experience)

I'm just sitting here at a patio table on the second floor of the college, campus.

My pencil seems heavy and horribly.

My writing paper appears to have no color.

My surroundings are all but nondescript.

I'm seeing people—yet, I'm not really seeing them.

I'm hearing things—and, it's all sounding just like yackety-yak.

Even the surrounding vegetation seems in-consequential and in-visible.

I'm making mistakes in my writing—why?

I'll tell you why, soon, enough.

The sky's turning a darkly gray-blue, and the air's getting much cooler.

People are passing by slowly—passing by tiredly.

I'm seeing some birds flying all about the wide-open roof.

Their color and shape and even style are all un-known to me.

Everything is just a great big blur—or, almost meaning-less—and, why?

It's because I'm tired and sleepy and even un-able to think completely.

# A Pretty Pleasurable Cigarette

Long and thin and good and bad;
Expensive yet pleasurable but not always:
Smelly and messy but oh how it gives such gratification—or, pleasure, if only too damn
Temporary….
A pretty pleasurable cigarette…?
No, yes, well—perhaps, all right—it's a dangerously dark pleasure.
And, a habit, or, a bad habit—yes, no, well—quite possibly…:
Bad and good and thin and even long—or, so long—long on smell and taste but short on
Pleasure.
Oh, well, no—yes—most probably…!

## Sinking Heart

That's so right; on any day or night, it'll nev'r find the child: Sad-ness.

Oh no!

As her parents' life hasn't any bad-ness.

Oh yes! Such is important to know.

In fact, the family's good life just fills their thick, high, and wide cheeks with much

Red-ness and glad-ness….

## Black Flower

Sitting next to the officers' pool on a forsaken island
And peering at the colorfully greenish-blue Caribbean Sea
Its color so colorful—or gorgeous—like the azurean sky
The golden sun casting, gorgeously, reflections of glittery diamonds upon delicate waves
The sound of such waves breaking up—super sweet sounding
The ocean's saltily fresh smell clearing my mind of all cloudily dark thoughts
The circularly crisp feel of early autumn giving me a sense of brand new hope
At this instant, whilst sitting next to the officers' pool on a fantastically forsaken island
I make a promise to myself
A promise that's *just* as sweet as brown sugar and as beautiful as a poisonously
Black Flower
That's rather tasty and mellifluous in all of its Half-Empty joy and sorrow.

## Good Name

Others often try not to reach one of life's most sought after stations.

    Because, it's a certain elevation that's very much weight'd.

Per chance, that's why some just avoid certain temptations;

        To ensure with certainty that their fates won't ev'r be frustrat'd.

    Nor should I've to translate such utterly universal translations:

This is to say, who among us doesn't desire Honor—or, a greatly good name;

Whose high station in life often-times afford few a high standing in life's giant game:

        It's quite simply all about the good versus the bad.

Just, the same, that one would've had to been tam'd; to suffer some pretty proper pain;

To avoid some sort of starkly dark stain—un-less, she or he is so mad as to be had.

    That's right, Old Man; for, I'm only too goddamn glad that you'll nev'r live to be my damn dad!

# Beautiful Death
(A Dedication to Pain & Suffering—Misery)


He'd lived a life in an un-bearable world:
It was a world of eye-opening darkness and dreadful disappointment.
He'd often pursued a peace of mind,
While all the time his composure bordered on the line of turmoil.
He'd searched long and hard for lasting health—yet,
For his efforts, he was left heart-sickened.
He'd often sought lasting love—but, he was met with constant heart-break.
He'd often sought humble happiness—success; and, what he got was—well, dis-content.
So, it'd been on one dark, depressive, devastative day, morning, and afternoon;
And even evening, which he no longer wanted to live in a demandingly demonic world.
He'd told all of this no one—except, to himself in the privacy of his *own* living hell.
Help. Help! Help?
It was something that he'd known was available; still, it remained elusive, and, very.
Yes, absolutely! He'd entertained the whole idea of death (or suicide).
He'd to just end the mean madness and all the super sick sadness!
While the joy of it all was that he'd no shame, no, not none…!
Oh, yes! Death is so—oh—so beautiful!
It's quite un-like that utterly un-bearable world; that, he'd known only too damn well:
It was a world of eye-opening darkness and dreadful disappointment.
It's now in death that he's able to live a beautifully bearable life.
It's in death, as well, that he's ultimately able to grasp—forever:
Or, clasp long-lasting peace, health, love, happiness, and success, and even eternal rest.
Finally, to all those who he's left behind—since, I want you-all to know: That, through
Death, he's now realized and relished the essence of life, and roundly.
Thank you, and, oh—he so thanks you…! Most Beautiful Death!

## Ill-Repute

It's something that the doggedly hard-working woman can't—or, won't tolerate—
Disgrace.
Such has almost always been the case even though others in life's big fat race have sought, so endlessly, to debase her greatly good name.
Yet, the woman almost certainly moves with haste in keeping up the gritty pace;
Since, she almost nev'r tolerates any waste.
For it's no shame, as it's just how such has to be play'd: life's big fat game.
That's so right; the woman wouldn't bear any loss lest she changes or lessens her taste.

# Afterthought

Is mixed poetry best?

    I personally think so. This is to say, that it can be good if not great, to create a mixture of fixed and un-fixed poems. The former—fixed is rhymed like a sonnet, and the latter—un-fixed is un-rhymed like free-verse. Poetically, to be able to write various poems, schematically, stylistically, and randomly, without regard; to some set rule(s), is truly, what poeticizing is all about. In other words, to be able to just use one's "poetic license," so using all conventionally and un-conventionally poetic devices; to effectuate a certain affect/effect, in conveying thoughts and feelings either loftily or impassionately and imaginatively—freely; all of which, makes for some interesting if not some unique poems.

    Such is true, especially, in the case of creating free-verse poetry or even prose-poetry. That does not conform, so necessarily, to certain kinds of rhymes or the mixture thereof: masculine; feminine; slant; perfect; or, rhyme schemes—aa, aba, abab, ababa, ababab…; poems: couplets—aa, bb, cc, dd, ee…; terza rimes—aba, bcb, cdc, ded, efe…; quatrains—abab, cdcd, efef, ghgh, ijij…; or, even, varied sonnets—typically, 14 lines of poetry, as, in a Shakespearean sonnet: abab, cdcd, efef, gg; Petrarchan (Italian) sonnet—abbaabba, cdecde; Spenserian sonnet—abab, bcbc, cdcd, ee; none of which, once again, conforms, so necessarily, to free-verse poetry, or even prose-poetry. Withstanding such, what about form and rhythm; both of which—rhythm, form—are almost, always, seen in fixed poems?

    We ought to question such question with another/other question(s): Why forgo if not sacrifice a riddle, a narrative, or a confessional, or even a catalog poem, and so forth; to achieve some set form or rhythm, poetically? Why discard, or rather, disregard, and, down-rightly, such poetic tools as stream of consciousness, meditation, enjambment, or automatic writing, and so on; to just achieve some set rhythm or form, poetically? In the end—or, final analysis, what is the very big trade-off of not metering some poem; whose metrical lines may or may not afford some poet some pretty poetic liberty, or lots of latitude, very poetically? I surmise, or submit, too, that such final question will remain, forever, questionable. Still, why not indulge or benefit from such mixture of poetry, for now?

www.ingramcontent.com/pod-product-compliance
Lightning Source LLC
Chambersburg PA
CBHW081021040426
42444CB00014B/3305